J   Roesler, Jill
940
.5425 Eyewitness to dropping
ROE   of the atomic bombs

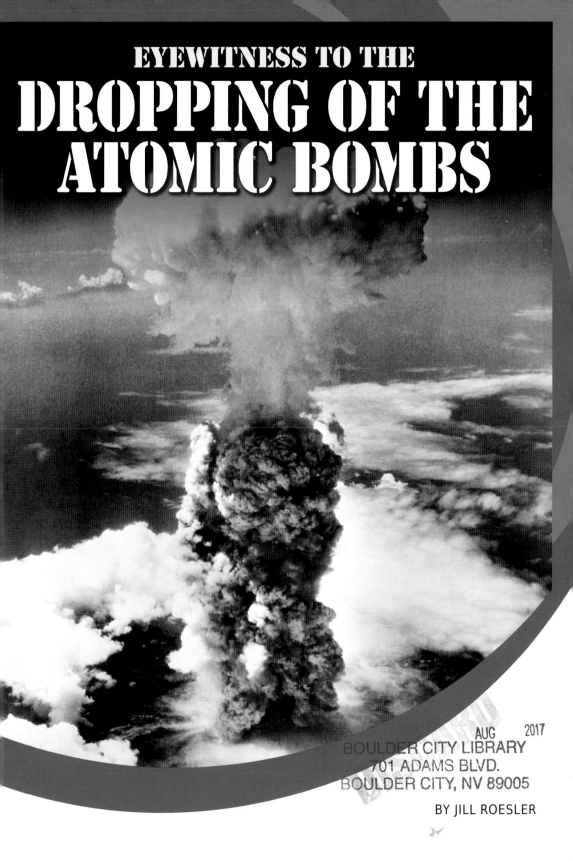

EYEWITNESS TO THE
DROPPING OF THE
ATOMIC BOMBS

BY JILL ROESLER

Published by The Child's World®
1980 Lookout Drive • Mankato, MN 56003-1705
800-599-READ • www.childsworld.com

Acknowledgments
The Child's World®: Mary Berendes, Publishing Director
Red Line Editorial: Design, editorial direction, and production
Photographs ©: SuperStock/Corbis, cover, 1; Everett Historical/Shutterstock Images,
4, 10, 15, 16, 20, 26, 29; Corbis, 7, 22; Orren Jack Turner/Library of Congress, 8;
Bettmann/Corbis, 12; George R. Caron/U.S. Air Force/AP Images, 19; AP Images, 25

ISBN 9781634074162

LCCN 2015946230

Printed in the United States of America
Mankato, MN
December, 2015
PA02281

ABOUT THE AUTHOR

Jill Roesler is from southern Minnesota. In addition to writing children's
books, she writes for several newspapers. Her favorite subject to research
and write about is history. In her free time, Roesler enjoys reading, traveling,
and gardening.

TABLE OF
CONTENTS

Chapter 1

CREATING THE BOMBS

On August 6, 1945, the *Enola Gay* bomber plane rose into the sky. The plane carried a crew of 10 U.S. military men. It also held a bomb that weighed 8,900 pounds (4,037 kg). The crew members had been on many **air raids**. But this voyage was different.

"We're going on a bombing mission, but it's a little bit special," Colonel Paul Tibbets told the crew. Tibbets was flying the plane.

"Colonel, we wouldn't be playing with **atoms** today, would we?" asked Bob Caron, a crew member.

"Bob, you've got it exactly right," said Tibbets. "This is an atom bomb we're dropping."[1] The men listened silently. They understood the seriousness of the mission.

The United States had been at war with Japan and Germany for nearly four years. Many other nations were involved in the conflict. World War II had caused millions of deaths and injuries around the world. In May 1945, Germany surrendered to the United States and its allies. But the United States was still at war with Japan.

"I knew that it would end the war and that in doing so it would save very many American lives."

—*Vannevar Bush, head of the U.S. Office of Scientific Research and Development during World War II, on the atomic bomb*[2]

The ten-man crew of the *Enola Gay* was part of a drastic mission to end the war.

The *Enola Gay* was carrying an atomic bomb. The bomb was the most destructive weapon in history. It was made from an element called uranium. This element can produce large amounts of energy. Through the process of **nuclear fission**, scientists can split a uranium atom into lighter atoms. This process creates a chemical reaction of enormous destructive power.

On that August morning, the plane soared above Hiroshima, Japan. The crew prepared to drop the bomb. Government officials hoped that the bomb would bring a quick surrender from Japan. But it would also kill tens of thousands of people. American leaders had faced a difficult choice. The bomb would change the world forever.

The mission to create an atomic bomb started years earlier. In 1938, two Austrian physicists discovered nuclear fission. The war had not yet begun. But Germany was building up its military force. Some scientists worried that Germany could use nuclear fission to develop powerful new weapons.

Physicist Albert Einstein was deeply concerned. In the 1930s, he moved from Germany to the United States. Einstein feared that Germany was using uranium to develop atomic bombs. Another physicist, Leó Szilárd, urged him to contact the U.S.

▲ The crew of the *Enola Gay* posed for a photograph before takeoff.

government. On August 2, 1939, the scientists wrote a letter to President Franklin Roosevelt. They warned of the threat of atomic weapons. Einstein and Szilárd urged the president to contact scientists who studied nuclear fission. That way, if Germany developed a dangerous weapon, the United States could fight back.

The president received a lot of mail. Einstein wanted someone to deliver the letter in person. For months, he tried to find someone to deliver it. Einstein worried that time was running

▲ Scientist Albert Einstein encouraged the government to research atomic bombs.

out. Finally, Einstein's friend Alexander Sachs arranged a meeting with the president. Sachs read the letter aloud. The president sat silently for a moment. Then he declared, "This requires action."[3]

In October 1939, Roosevelt formed the Advisory Committee on Uranium (ACU). The group included military officials and scientists. The ACU started a top-secret program called the Manhattan Project. The project had two leaders: Leslie Groves and Robert Oppenheimer. Groves was a gruff army colonel. Oppenheimer was a brilliant, sometimes mysterious scientist. The two men often argued. But they had a deep respect for one another. Together, they made plans to build the first atomic bomb.

Oppenheimer swiftly put together a group of scientists. They included experts from all over the world. Secrecy was very important. Manhattan Project scientists lived in Los Alamos, New Mexico. This area was almost completely cut off from the rest of the country. Scientists were forbidden to tell anyone where they worked. They all shared a single post-office box for mail. Army guards watched for intruders.

Los Alamos was not on any maps. Some called it the Secret City. The city was surrounded by steep, rocky cliffs. The high peaks hid the location from view. Oppenheimer chose the location himself. He hoped its beauty would inspire the scientists.

Oppenheimer's scientists worked day and night. By the summer of 1945, they were ready to test the first atomic bomb.

Chapter 2

TRUMAN'S DECISION

While scientists developed the bomb, the war raged on. Germany surrendered on May 7, 1945. Americans cheered for the end of the war in Europe. Parades marched down many city streets. But the United States and its allies still battled the Japanese army.

By then, the war seemed to be in its final stages. Japanese forces had suffered many losses.

But they were loyal to the emperor of Japan, Hirohito. Soldiers fought according to an ancient Japanese code. The code said that dying for one's country was nobler than losing a war. Military leaders in Japan refused to surrender. Each month, thousands of U.S. and Japanese troops were dying.

Many U.S. authorities believed that drastic measures were needed to end the war. Roosevelt had considered using atomic bombs on Japan. But in April 1945, Roosevelt became sick and died. The task of deciding whether to drop the bombs fell to the new president, Harry S. Truman.

Truman was known as a smart, practical man. Still, he struggled to adjust to his new responsibilities. "I felt like the moon, the stars, and all the planets had fallen on me," he said.[4] Truman had not known about the top-secret Manhattan Project. Unexpectedly, he faced a difficult decision.

Truman met with Leslie Groves and Secretary of War Henry Stimson. The men told him about their efforts to create an atomic bomb. Truman knew that the bomb would be incredibly destructive. He called it "the most terrible thing ever discovered."[5] The bomb would kill many **civilians**. Even survivors

▲ President Truman (left) talked with
Secretary of War Henry Stimson.

would have serious injuries. Stimson said that atomic bombs
could destroy the world.

Still, Stimson argued that the bomb was Truman's best option.
Its destruction could convince Japanese leaders to surrender.
Without the bomb, the war might last for months or even years.
Large numbers of people would die. Stimson said an atomic
bomb could prevent those deaths.

Soon after this meeting, scientists with the Manhattan Project
gathered for an important experiment. They **detonated** an

atomic weapon in New Mexico. Scientists chose an abandoned area in the desert. It was far from any towns. Oppenheimer named the experiment the Trinity Test.

The research team dropped the test bomb on a large steel tower. A bright flash of light lit up the morning sky. A fireball shot high into the air. It created a **mushroom cloud**. The cloud stretched 40,000 feet (12,192 m) into the sky. The steel tower turned into vapor.

Scientists watched the explosion from a safe area. They were amazed by what they saw. "It was like being at the bottom of an ocean of light," said Joan Hinton.

"We knew the world would not be the same. A few people laughed, a few people cried, most people were silent."

—*Robert Oppenheimer on the Trinity Test*[6]

She was one of the few female scientists at Los Alamos. Hinton said the explosion "turned purple and blue. . . . Then suddenly the sound reached us. It was very sharp and rumbled and all the mountains were rumbling with it."[7]

Groves and Oppenheimer were pleased with the test. But some scientists grew concerned. They believed that atomic bombs should be used only as a last resort. Seventy scientists from the Manhattan Project signed a letter to Truman. They asked him to consider the dangers of the atomic bomb. However, Truman had made up his mind. He told military officials to prepare to drop two bombs on Japan. If needed, scientists would make more bombs.

On July 26, Truman met with the leaders of Britain and China, two U.S. allies. They issued the Potsdam Declaration. This document urged Japanese forces to surrender. If they did not, they would face "utter destruction."[8] Japanese leaders gave no response. Less than two weeks later, the *Enola Gay* plane took off. On board was an atomic bomb with the code name "Little Boy."

During the Trinity Test, scientists detonated ▶
the first atomic bomb.

Chapter 3

DROPPING THE BOMB

It was 2:00 a.m. on August 6. The *Enola Gay* was waiting on the tiny Pacific island of Tinian. Colonel Tibbets boarded the plane. He was startled to see cameras flashing. Truman had asked photographers to capture the moment.

By 2:15 a.m., the men were on their way. The flight took about six hours. By 8:15 a.m., they spotted their target area. The plane soared 26,000 feet (7,925 m) above Hiroshima. "One second!" Tibbets yelled.[9] That was the signal to drop the bomb. The crew launched the weapon. The airplane lurched. Little Boy fell to the ground.

It was a sunny day in Hiroshima. Many Japanese citizens were at work in factories. Others were at home. "The morning [was] still, warm, and beautiful," said Dr. Michihiko Hachiya.[10] The doctor had worked late the night before. At 8:15 a.m., he was lying in his bed. Half-asleep, he watched shadows move in his garden. Suddenly, Hachiya saw a blinding flash of light. Then another bright light flashed. The bomb had detonated over Hiroshima.

Hachiya watched his roof begin to crumble. He found that he was bleeding. Bits of glass had cut his skin. He called out to his wife, Yaeko. She was also bleeding and confused. Dazed, the couple stumbled out of their house. The Hachiyas had survived the bombing. But many of their neighbors did not. The bomb turned buildings and people to ash almost instantly. It destroyed all buildings within an area of 5 square miles (13 sq. km). A mushroom cloud rose 60,000 feet (18,000 m) high. The city of Hiroshima was almost completely wiped out.

"Nothing remained except a few buildings of reinforced concrete," said Hachiya. "The city was like a desert except for scattered piles of brick and roof tile."[11]

Nearly 80,000 people died in the blast. Another 35,000 people were injured. Many had serious burns and bruises. Thousands more died within the next few years. Exposure to **radiation** made them very ill. The bomb had caused incredible destruction. But this was only the first bomb. Scientists had built two bombs to drop on Japan. American leaders waited to see if Japan would surrender. If Japan did not, they would drop the second bomb.

"I had a feeling that all the human beings on the face of the earth had been killed off, and only the five of us were left behind."

—a fifth-grade boy in Hiroshima who was with his family when the bomb hit[12]

When the atomic bomb detonated, smoke rose thousands of ▶ feet into the air.

18

Chapter 4

THE SECOND BOMB

News of the bombing traveled quickly. That evening, Truman gave a radio address to all Americans. He gravely announced that U.S. forces had dropped a bomb on the city of Hiroshima. The president urged Japanese forces to surrender. If they did not, he said, the United States would drop more bombs.

In Japan, military officials fiercely debated what action to take. Some doubted that the United

◀ The atomic bomb destroyed the area around the Museum of Science and Industry in Hiroshima.

States could make more than one bomb. They did not believe Truman's threats. Emperor Hirohito disagreed. On August 8, he told advisers that he wanted to end the war as quickly as possible. But by then, U.S. plans were underway to drop another atomic bomb.

That same day, Colonel Tibbets met with other U.S. military officials. They discussed where to drop the second bomb. The officials chose the ancient city of Kokura, by the sea. This city was home to a large weapons factory.

Early in the morning of August 9, Major Charles Sweeney and his crew boarded the *Bockscar* plane. The plane took off from Tinian at 3:49 a.m. On board was an atomic bomb with the code name "Fat Man." This massive bomb was even heavier than Little Boy. Fat Man weighed nearly 10,000 pounds (4,536 kg).

Almost seven hours after takeoff, the plane reached its target. But thick clouds of smoke filled the sky above Kokura. A nearby town had been firebombed the day before. Fires still blazed on the ground below. Crew members could hardly see through the smoke. Sweeney flew past the target three times. But the heavy clouds did not clear.

The crew had a backup plan. Sweeney flew to the nearby city of Nagasaki. There, too, clouds blanketed the sky. Suddenly, though, the sky cleared. Crew member Captain Kermit Beahan spotted the target for the bomb.

"The target was there, pretty as a picture," said Beahan. "I made the run, let the bomb go."[13] At 11:02 a.m., the *Bockscar* released the atomic bomb.

At a nearby military outpost, Japanese soldiers had noticed the U.S. plane flying overhead. They sounded an air-raid siren. Michie Hattori, age 15, was at school when she heard the siren. She hurried to a bomb shelter. "I ran as fast as I could," Hattori said. "I . . . made it to the shelter ahead of the rest of my class."[15]

Hattori stood at the entrance to the shelter. She urged the other girls to get inside. But it was too late. Hattori saw a flash

> "Suddenly, the light of a thousand suns illuminated the cockpit. . . . I had never experienced such an intense light, maybe three or four times brighter than the sun shining above us."
>
> —*Fred J. Olivi, co-pilot of the* Bockscar[14]

◀ **Emperor Hirohito considered surrendering to the United States after the first atomic bomb was dropped.**

of bright light. Then she felt a sudden burning feeling. The girls outside the shelter cried out. Many had burns or broken bones.

The bomb wiped out 2.6 square miles (6.7 sq. km) of the city. More than 40,000 people were killed. Buildings crumbled all over Nagasaki. Fires broke out in the streets. The damage could have been even greater. Nagasaki was surrounded by mountains. The mountains stopped the blast from traveling beyond the city.

"The people . . . ran about like so many ants seeking to escape," said Tatsuichiro Akizuki, a doctor in Nagasaki. "It seemed like the end of the world."[16] The second atomic bomb had been dropped. Allied troops were also making gains on the ground in Japan. U.S. forces waited to see if Japan would surrender.

A man examined the rubble in a Nagasaki ▶ neighborhood after the bombing.

Chapter 5

THE END OF THE WAR

After the second bombing, Emperor Hirohito called an emergency meeting of the Japanese War Council. The council debated for hours. Some commanders still wanted to continue the war. But by 2:00 a.m., the emperor had made his decision. He convinced the council that it was time to surrender.

"Continuing the war can only end in the **annihilation** of the Japanese people," he declared.[17]

On August 15, 1945, Emperor Hirohito spoke to his people on the radio. For many people, it was the first time they had heard the emperor's voice. He announced his surrender. "This is the day we have been waiting for," President Truman said.[18] Two weeks later, officials from Japan, the United States, and other nations met on the USS *Missouri*. The U.S. flag fluttered in the wind. Flags of U.S. allies were also on display. The leaders signed papers to make Japan's surrender official. Some people in the crowd wept.

At home, Americans celebrated their victory. People sang songs and danced in the streets. The war was finally over. But the use of atomic bombs brought new fears. Over the years, victims suffered effects from the atomic bombs. Scientists are still studying the effects of atomic bomb radiation.

Several scientists regretted creating such a powerful weapon. Albert Einstein said that the bombs created a "dreadful danger for all mankind."[19] General Dwight D. Eisenhower was a commander of the Allied forces. He asked if the bombings were needed. "The Japanese were ready to surrender," he said. "It wasn't necessary to hit them with that awful thing."[20] But others maintained that the atomic bombs had prevented further battles.

President Truman believed that dropping the bombs was right and even merciful.

Einstein worried that more nations would develop atomic bombs. Nuclear wars would threaten the future of humankind. Some of his fears came true. By 1952, Britain and the Soviet Union had created nuclear weapons. Today, nine nations have these weapons.

Leaders of many nations wanted nuclear weapons for protection. But they recognized the dangers. Countries signed **treaties** to prevent the use of these weapons. One was the 1968 Treaty on the Non-Proliferation of Nuclear Weapons. This treaty said that no more nations could develop nuclear weapons.

As the years passed, some people who were in Hiroshima and Nagasaki during the bombing became very ill. Survivors of the bombing suffered from cancer and other ailments. The events in Hiroshima and Nagasaki showed the dangerous power of atomic bombs. Since World War II, no nation has used nuclear weapons against an enemy.

Months after the atomic bombing, buildings in Hiroshima ▶ were still in ruins.

GLOSSARY

air raids (AIR RAIDZ): During air raids, attackers drop bombs from airplanes. The U.S. military often conducted air raids on Japan.

annihilation (uh-nahy-uh-LAY-shun): Annihilation is complete destruction. Emperor Hirohito feared the annihilation of Japan in the war.

atoms (AT-uhmz): Atoms are very small parts of matter. Scientists use uranium atoms to create the Little Boy atomic bomb.

civilians (si-VIL-yunz): Civilians are people who are not in the military. Atomic bombs can kill or injure civilians.

detonated (DET-uhn-ayt-ed): When something is detonated, it explodes. Scientists detonated a test bomb in New Mexico.

mushroom cloud (MUSH-room KLOWD): A mushroom cloud is a large mass of smoke from a nuclear explosion. After the Hiroshima bombing, a mushroom cloud formed.

nuclear fission (NOO-klee-er FISH-un): Nuclear fission is the act of splitting an atom into smaller, lighter atoms. Nuclear fission is used to create atomic bombs.

radiation (ray-dee-AY-shun): In radiation, energy moves in the form of particles or waves. Some forms of radiation are dangerous.

treaties (TREE-teez): Treaties are official agreements between countries. Different nations have signed treaties about nuclear weapons.

SOURCE NOTES

1. Studs Terkel. "One Hell of a Big Bang." *The Guardian*. Guardian News and Media Ltd., 6 August 2002. Web. 25 June 2015.

2. Dennis D. Wainstock. *The Decision to Drop the Atomic Bomb*. New York: Enigma, 2013. Print. 64.

3. Walter Isaacson. "Chain Reaction: From Einstein to the Atomic Bomb." *Discover Magazine*. Kalmbach Publishing, 18 March 2008. Web. 25 June 2015.

4. "Thoughts of a President, 1945." *Eyewitness to History*. Ibis Communications, n.d. Web. 25 June 2015.

5. "Understanding the Decision to Drop the Bomb on Hiroshima and Nagasaki." *CSIS.org*. Center for Strategic and International Studies, 10 August 2012. Web. 25 June 2015.

6. "J. Robert Oppenheimer 'Now I am become death . . .'" *AtomicArchive.com*. National Science Digital Library, n.d. Web. 20 June 2015.

7. "Trinity Test – 1945." *Atomic Heritage Foundation*. Atomic Heritage Foundation, n.d. Web. 25 June 2015.

8. Harry S. Truman. "Statement by the President of the United States." *American Experience*. PBS, n.d. Web. 20 June 2015.

9. Studs Terkel. 6 August 2002.

10-11. "The Bombing of Hiroshima, 1945." *Eyewitness to History*. Ibis Communications, 2001. Web. 20 June 2015.

12. "Using the Atomic Bomb – 1945." *Atomic Heritage Foundation*. Atomic Heritage Foundation, n.d. Web. 25 June 2015.

13. Juan Gonzalez. "The Atomic Bombers Speak." *Democracy Now*. Democracy Now, 5 August 2005. Web. 25 June 2015.

14. "Using the Atomic Bomb – 1945." n.d.

15. "Eyewitness to the Nagasaki Bomb Blast." *HistoryNet*. World History Group, LLC, 12 June 2006. Web. 25 June 2015.

16. "Using the Atomic Bomb – 1945." n.d.

17-18. "This Day in History: Atomic Bomb Dropped on Nagasaki." *The History Channel*. A&E Television Networks, n.d. Web. 20 June 2015.

19. Albert Einstein. "On My Participation in the Atomic Bomb Project." *Atomic Archive*. AJ Software & Media, n.d. Web. 20 June 2015.

20. Mark Weber. "Was Hiroshima Necessary?" *The Journal of Historical Review*. Institute for Historical Review, 1997. Web. 20 June 2015.

TO LEARN MORE

Books

Baxter, Roberta. *The Dropping of the Atomic Bombs*. Ann Arbor, MI: Cherry Lake, 2014.

Ross, Stewart. *Hiroshima*. London: Arcturus, 2011.

Sheinkin, Steve. *Bomb: The Race to Build—and Steal—the World's Most Dangerous Weapon*. New York: Square Fish, 2012.

Web Sites

Visit our Web site for links about the dropping of the atomic bombs: childsworld.com/links

Note to Parents, Teachers, and Librarians: We routinely verify our Web links to make sure they are safe and active sites. So encourage your readers to check them out!

INDEX